STUDIES IN ECONOMIC AND SOCIAL HISTORY

This series, specially commissioned by the Economic History Society, provides a guide to the current interpretations of the key themes of economic and social history in which advances have recently been made or in which there has been significant debate.

Originally entitled 'Studies in Economic History', in 1974 the series had its scope extended to include topics in social history, and the new series title, 'Studies in Economic and Social History', signalises this development.

The series gives readers access to the best work done, helps them to draw their own conclusions in major fields of study, and by means of the critical bibliography in each book guides them in the selection of further reading. The aim is to provide a springboard to further work rather than a set of pre-packaged conclusions or short-cuts.

ECONOMIC HISTORY SOCIETY

The Economic History Society, which numbers over 3000 members, publishes the *Economic History Review* four times a year (free to members) and holds an annual conference. Enquiries about membership should be addressed to the Assistant Secretary, Economic History Society, Peterhouse, Cambridge. Full-time students may join the Society at special rates.

D0181817

STUDIES IN ECONOMIC AND SOCIAL HISTORY

Edited for the Economic History Society by M. W. Flinn

OTHER TITLES ARE IN PREPARATION

The Economic Effects of the Two World Wars on Britain

Prepared for
The Economic History Society by

ALAN S. MILWARD

Professor of European Studies
University of Manchester Institute of
Science and Technology

M

First edition 1970
Reprinted 1973, 1977

Published by
THE MACMILLAN PRESS LTD
London and Basingstoke
Associated companies in New York Dublin
Melbourne Johannesburg and Madras

ISBN 0 333 10262 2

Printed in Hong Kong by
C.T.P.S.

Contents

Acknowledgements

A work of this kind cannot pretend to any originality, but the form which it took persuaded me how much it owed to my former colleagues, Professor M. W. Flinn, Dr T. C. Smout and Professor S. B. Saul. When I had written it it seemed only right that they should read it. They all very kindly did so, thereby making it even more their own work.

Preface

SO long as the study of economic history was confined to only a small group at a few universities, its literature was not prolific and its few specialists had no great problem in keeping abreast of the work of their colleagues. Even in the 1930s there were only two journals devoted exclusively to this field. But the high quality of the work of the economic historians during the inter-war period and the post-war growth in the study of the social sciences sparked off an immense expansion in the study of economic history after the Second World War. There was a great expansion of research and many new journals were launched, some specialising in branches of the subject like transport, business or agricultural history. Most significantly, economic history began to be studied as an aspect of history in its own right in schools. As a consequence, the examining boards began to offer papers in economic history at all levels, while textbooks specifically designed for the school market began to be published.

For those engaged in research and writing this period of rapid expansion of economic history studies has been an exciting, if rather breathless one. For the larger numbers, however, labouring in the outfield of the schools and colleges of further education, the excitement of the explosion of research has been tempered by frustration caused by its vast quantity and, frequently, its controversial character. Nor, it must be admitted, has the ability or willingness of the academic economic historians to generalise and summarise marched in step with their enthusiasm for research.

The greatest problems of interpretation and generalisation have tended to gather round a handful of principal themes in economic history. It is, indeed, a tribute to the sound sense of economic historians that they have continued to dedicate their energies, however inconclusively, to the solution of these key problems. The results of this activity, however, much of it stored away in a wide range of academic journals, have tended to remain inaccessible to many of those currently interested in the subject. Recognising the need for guidance through the burgeoning and

7

confusing literature that has grown around these basic topics, the Economic History Society decided to launch this series of small books. The books are intended to serve as guides to current interpretations in important fields of economic history in which important advances have recently been made, or in which there has recently been some significant debate. Each book aims to survey recent work, to indicate the full scope of the particular problem as it has been opened up by recent scholarship, and to draw such conclusions as seem warranted, given the present state of knowledge and understanding. The authors will often be at pains to point out where, in their view, because of a lack of information or inadequate research, they believe it is premature to attempt to draw firm conclusions. While authors will not hesitate to review recent and older work critically, the books are not intended to serve as vehicles for their own specialist views: the aim is to provide a balanced summary rather than an exposition of the author's own viewpoint. Each book will include a descriptive bibliography.

In this way the series aims to give all those interested in economic history at a serious level access to recent scholarship in some major fields. Above all, the aim is to help the reader to draw his own conclusions, and to guide him in the selection of further reading as a means to this end, rather than to present him with a set of pre-packaged conclusions.

University of Edinburgh   M. W. FLINN
June 1968   *Editor*

8

The Subject

THE two world wars obtrude with stark obviousness into the history of Britain in this century. Their overwhelming reality has led historians to relate to them, directly or indirectly, an astonishing number of historical developments. The difference in economic organisation and in social life between wartime and peacetime has been so huge and so encapsulated in the personal consciousness of so many still alive that the wish to produce a comprehensive theory of the relationship between war and history starts from the soil turned by even the most aridly statistical of labourers. It is to these theories as they relate to the history of the British economy in this century that this pamphlet is directed. What changes in the economy have historians and economists laid to the account of the two world wars? And what changes may justly so be laid?

At the outset appears a methodological problem of no great complexity. So great was the economic effort needed to win both wars that while those wars were being fought, and under the pressure of fighting them, on each occasion the economy was quite transformed from what it had been in peacetime. The aim was to win, in the Second World War to win no matter what the cost. Therefore the main economic priority was to produce the necessary quantity of goods to defeat the enemy. Consequently the ultimate economic purpose was quite different from that of peacetime, and the kind of economy which was created has come to be known loosely by the term 'war economy'. The term is a loose one, for it is a matter of historical fact that most of the 'war economies' which have existed have neither had such simple priorities as, nor much resemblance to, the war economies which existed in Britain. It may even be questioned whether historians have not exaggerated the degree of unanimity of purpose which informed the economy in Britain during the two world wars. Nevertheless it must be stated that it is a matter of almost universal agreement that the British nation twice bent its united energies to creating an economy whose dominating purpose was to defeat the enemy, sweeping aside, gradually in the First World

9

War, and almost from the beginning in the Second, all other claims on that economy.

The result of this apparent clarity of purpose was to create a form of economic organisation for the duration of the war which was sharply different from that of the preceding and succeeding periods of peace. Those changes in the economy and in society which took place during the war and only for its duration, or for not very long afterwards, the short-term changes, will not concern us very much here. They are not the subject of controversy except in their more minute details. Indeed they have been described in such detail, with government help, for the Second World War as effectively to stop all but the most interested of historians from considering them at all. There are many perfectly adequate summaries in textbooks and the like of what the short-term changes in the economy were.[1] We may therefore resolve our methodological difficulty by concentrating on the more controversial problem of the long-term changes in the economy brought about by war in this century, considering the short-term changes only when necessary and in this wider context.

It is as well that we should be able so to simplify the issue. For the opinions about these long-term trends are often rather vague, differing enormously in their ultimate implications, but sometimes having a quite misleading resemblance to each other. The differences between them reflect the changes in British society, and in the way we have come to think about that society, over the last fifty years. For that reason they are considered first in roughly chronological order. They represent a set of changing concepts, each concept a framework wherein the actual historical events and economic facts may be fitted more or less successfully.

[1] That there is general agreement on these matters can be seen by comparing the accounts of the Second World War in S. Pollard, *The Development of the British Economy, 1914–1950* (1962) and A. J. Youngson, *Britain's Economic Growth, 1920–1966* (1967), two books written from different political standpoints. W. Ashworth, *An Economic History of England, 1870–1939* (1960) has a most comprehensive account of the First World War.

Its Changing Interpretation

FROM the second quarter of the eighteenth century economists evolved the idea that war was an almost unmitigated economic disaster. By the end of the century that view had become almost generally established and, excepting the notable dissent of Malthus, it remained more or less unchanged in Britain until the outbreak of the First World War. The earliest writers to consider the impact of that war on the economy took, therefore, an unrelievedly gloomy view of its results. They would have echoed what was already becoming received opinion when Samuel Johnson published, in 1749, his imitation of Juvenal's tenth Satire:

> Yet Reason frowns on War's unequal Game,
> Where wasted Nations raise a single Name,
> And mortgag'd States their Grandsires' Wreaths regret,
> From Age to Age in everlasting Debt.[1]

Many of them did indeed afterwards echo this idea almost exactly. 'Thus the Great War', wrote Hirst and Allen in 1928, 'brought a load of debt, taxes and misery incalculable. The expenditure during the four years that it lasted reached a total incomprehensible and inconceivable to the ordinary mind.'[2]

This interpretation, which we may call the classical liberal interpretation, saw war in relatively simple terms as a loss. However complex the event, the net result was always a loss to the economy, of cash, of production, of capital and of people. R. H. Brand, himself a merchant banker, summarised this view in the series of analyses of government policy which he published throughout the First World War. 'They were not able to see that all this outpouring of our substance on the war was accompanied

---

[1] It was a completely eighteenth-century gloss on what Juvenal had written, which is more nearly rendered in Dryden's translation:
> Of every nation, each illustrious name,
> Such toys as these have cheated into fame;
> Exchanging solid quiet, to obtain
> The windy satisfaction of the brain.

[2] F. W. Hirst and J. E. Allen, *British War Budgets* (1928) p. 18.

by a constant deterioration of our economic situation, by a vast loss of national capital, and by the creation of a huge load of debt, internal and external – in fact that we were like a spendthrift, living more or less at our ease by wasting our capital.'[1] Although, he conceded, war on such a scale as the First World War represented an immense productive effort, what was produced was essentially 'non-productive wealth'. Meanwhile 'productive wealth' was being destroyed and capital was allowed to depreciate. The inflation accompanying the war was only disguising the fact that in the long run the country's productive capacity and purchasing power were being steadily reduced to the point where a depression would certainly be produced after the war. When that depression did arrive in 1920, Brand, and others who shared his standpoint, therefore blamed it on the war. That the depression of the 1920s was to be blamed directly or indirectly on the First World War was all too easy a deduction from the theoretical assumptions underlying this view of war. Lloyd George, introducing the first budget of the war, prophesied a brief period of prosperity at the end of the war followed by a severe industrial crisis. The most ardent, although not the most profound, advocate of this well-established interpretation was F. W. Hirst, whose book, *The Consequences of the War to Great Britain*, was published in 1934. He also categorised the depression of 1920 as being the 'automatic' result of the war, aggravated by the foolish policy pursued by the government of not raising a sufficient proportion of the war expenditure by higher taxation. Greater taxation would have meant less borrowing, less borrowing would have meant a less crippling public debt in the 1920s. 'The expenses of a war', said Gladstone, introducing the Crimean war budget to the House of Commons, 'are the moral check which it has pleased the Almighty to impose upon the ambition and the lust of conquest that are inherent in so many nations.' This, however, did not absolve the public from the duty to suffer the same moral chastisement when resisting an aggressor. The consequence of their refusal in 1914–18 was a burden of debt payments under which the 1920s foundered.

Since war was a loss, the only way its effects on the economy could be finally expressed was to calculate that loss as accurately as possible. Hirst and other writers sharing his liberal viewpoint

---

[1] R. H. Brand, *War and National Finance* (1921) p. 256.

therefore tried to add together the various elements of that loss and to 'cost' them. The effects of the First World War in their eyes could be expressed as what it had 'cost' the economy, or what sum of money would be sufficient to restore the economy to its previous state were that possible. However, whereas some elements of the total loss could be valued reasonably accurately without great difficulty, such as the value of the ships sunk and the cargo they contained, other elements were more elusive. The actual sum of money needed to pay for the war proved difficult to determine, and it was this problem which led Bogart, following the same interpretation as Hirst, to the notion that the total loss to the economy was compounded both of 'direct' and 'indirect' costs.[1]

The 'direct costs' comprised the physical destruction of capital due to enemy action. For Britain a considerable part of this was the loss of armaments and shipping, the damage to capital within the national frontier being very small. But at this stage of evaluation the knotty question arose of how to value the human capital destroyed by enemy action. The liberal writers were perfectly justified in facing up to this question in the way they did, even though to our eyes their proceedings may suggest a certain heartlessness, for within the concept of 'direct costs' the loss of people was so obvious a fact that it could not be dodged. From the outbreak of war to its close the British Army and Navy lost at least 616,382 men, excluding those of colonial or dominion nationality, through enemy action or other forms of death. Over the same period 1,656,735 men were wounded, some of them so seriously that they would never be able to work again. Most of these people were in the prime of their working life and the proportion of officers killed and wounded was higher than that of men.

In arriving at a value to ascribe to this particular item Bogart and Hirst relied very heavily on earlier work. Giffen had made an attempt to value the human beings lost in the Franco-Prussian War and the concepts which he there developed passed directly into the work of Bogart and Hirst.[2] Of course the Franco-Prussian War was a smaller affair, killing a mere 184,000 men and, to

[1] E. L. Bogart, *Direct and Indirect Costs of the Great World War* (1920).

[2] Sir R. Giffen, *Economic Inquiries and Studies* (1904) I 1–74.

complicate the matter further, those killed were a much more homogeneous group than those killed in the British armed forces between 1914 and 1918. Forty years of economic development had resulted in a greater variety of jobs in the economy and, when it is considered that conscription operated mainly on the basis of age and fitness, the problems of determining the average capital value of a dead soldier will readily be seen. The values on which Bogart and Hirst finally settled were derived from the calculations of a French actuary, Barriol, who had considered this problem. Where they differed from his sums they did so quite arbitrarily. Barriol attributed an average *per capita* value to the citizens of various potentially belligerent countries.[1] That is to say that a dead American soldier was a much greater loss to the economy than a dead Serbian soldier, since not only was he a piece of human capital who had been much more expensive to educate and train to the moment of his death, but his subsequent productive capacity, had he not died, would have been much greater. Barriol's figures were for all citizens. Working from them Bogart estimated the *per capita* value of a dead British soldier at $4,140, or $260 more than a dead German soldier, or more than twice the value of a dead Russian soldier. The elements in the calculation were the length of time the soldier would have been likely to live, the potential value of his lost labour, or the value of his potential savings plus his potential purchasing power plus his potential taxable capacity, and the cost to the state of supporting his family after his death or maiming.[2] The differences in value represent roughly the differences in the level of economic development of the countries concerned, the general conclusion being that the effect of war on a highly developed country such as Britain was likely to be much more serious than on an underdeveloped country.

To accept this method of procedure it is necessary to accept a number of hypotheses. These are, that it is possible to calculate an average duration of life which is valid for all, that it is possible to calculate a potential average net income of those killed or maimed which would embrace the very wide differences in social class which existed in the British armed forces, and that it is

[1] *Revue Économique Internationale*, Dec 1910 and May 1911.
[2] Whether these elements were all real costs or merely transfer payments was considered neither by Barriol nor his followers.

possible to calculate an average potential consumption and express it in monetary terms. Nor will the critic be slow to indicate that national product *per capita* is not the same as the income received by the population. Nor can it be argued that the 'cost' to the economy can be shown if the casualty's potential consumption be deducted from his potential production, for it is only true that the loss of a man equals a certain reduction in national product if there is full employment and if the conditions of work remain the same for the time span of the calculation, that is to say until he would have died. Had he been unemployed before the war the economy might actually have gained by his death, and there is little likelihood that, in whatever sector of production he had been employed, the production function in that sector would remain unchanged for a further thirty years. In addition there are the doubts cast on the procedure by demographic studies. Although so little comparative work on the demographic effects of war has been done that it is difficult to generalise, the birth-rate immediately after war appears to leap sharply, although temporarily, upwards.[1] There is evidence that, in this respect at least, the demographic 'loss' is not as great as might be assumed.

There is also a further difficulty which applies equally to the measurement of the 'indirect costs'. The relative value of the major currencies, which had remained more or less tied to each other for a long period, began to fluctuate wildly after 1914, so that no country's currency had the same purchasing power in 1918 as in 1914 and none retained the same relation to another. The unit of currency was therefore a rather unsatisfactory medium in which to evaluate the 'cost' of the war. In calculating 'indirect costs' Bogart's object was to arrive at a total of 'war expenses'. The sums of money officially allocated in 'war budgets' or raised by 'war loans' might not effectively be spent purely on the prosecution of the war. In any case the extension of the power of the government over economic life in constructing the 'war economy' of the First World War was so great that the whole scope and purpose of the budget changed in those years. Bogart therefore calculated an average annual level of peacetime expenditure and deducted this for five years from the actual

[1] See, for example, R. Easterlin, *The Postwar American Baby Boom in Historical Perspective*, National Bureau of Economic Research, Occasional Paper 79 (Princeton, 1962).

expenditure in the First World War, thus expressing the war expenses as $44,029,000,000.

It is easy to see the weaknesses in this method of procedure. Do the expenses of a war really begin with the declaration of war? And do they end when the fighting stops? What are 'normal' budgetary expenses? Jèze, who performed similar calculations for France, considered the 'war expenses' to be the difference in the public debt between the beginning and the end of war.[1] But the same questions must apply, apart from a further question about the size of the external debt. However, we are not so concerned here with those weaknesses as with the assumptions that fathered them. The nature of these assumptions can be simply revealed by posing a question that any economist would now pose. Is the extra expenditure entailed by war wholly a loss to the economy, or is some part of it actually beneficial in so far as it stimulates employment and production?

Yet the assumptions which underlay the classical liberal interpretation were the current intellectual coin not only of historians but of those who made policy. Although in such a war as the First World War it was inevitable that the government could not raise the whole 'cost' of the war from taxation but had to borrow money, the Chancellor of the Exchequer, McKenna, applied to this borrowing policy the rule which came to be known as the 'McKenna rule', not to borrow without imposing new taxation sufficient to provide for the interest on, and a sinking fund to reduce, the new loans. More serious than this, the whole idea of the 'cost' of war was embodied in the demand for reparations from Germany. And this demand, embodied in government policy throughout the 1920s, created such international economic havoc as to be one of the main and most disastrous consequences of the war itself.

The dramatic short-term changes during the First World War led many of those who were involved in them or who later studied them to reject the strict liberal interpretation as being too narrow. Out of such change something must survive, they argued. Indeed the events of the First World War, more than anything else, dealt a death-blow to the classical liberal tradition. The introduction of conscription, the full-time employment of a large part of the population that had not previously experienced regular

[1] G. Jèze, *Les Dépenses de guerre de la France* (Paris, 1926).

16

employment, the beginnings of aerial bomb attacks on civilians, the Allied blockade and Germany's unrestricted submarine warfare directly involved a far larger proportion of the population in the war than in other modern wars. In this light the liberal interpretation seemed insufficiently comprehensive to explain satisfactorily the impact of war on the economy. War was not only a loss, it was also a force for change, change which in some cases might be construed as gain.

From this paradox developed all subsequent interpretations. Their development reflects the greater concern of historians and economists with groups and with society as a whole rather than with individuals, and a move in social thought away from the mechanical accounting of Bogart to a concern with less strictly defined aspects of the human condition. In this change of outlook the world wars have played a dominating role, especially in Britain. Elsewhere interpretations of the kind put forward by Hirst survived up to and even during the Second World War. The volume of the *American Economic Review* for 1940 contains several articles in which the main effect of war is considered as its tendency to promote economic instability and to produce either a downturn in the trade cycle or a severe crisis outside the normal oscillations of that cycle.[1] That the major economies after the Second World War have experienced not instability but a most remarkable period of stability has lent particular force to the arguments of those that rejected the older liberal view, especially as the stability of the United States economy may have been increased by defence expenditure and even by the impact of the Korean War.[2]

The most important of the early movements to another interpretation was that of A. L. Bowley. His careful statistical analyses of the effects of the First World War have stood historians in good stead ever since and are a fine example of the superiority of research over opinion. For in his opinions Bowley differed scarcely a jot from Hirst, although his work repeatedly

[1] A similar view is expressed as late as 1945 in C. Rist, *Mécanismes économiques élémentaires* (Paris, 1945).

[2] See, for example, B. Hickman, *The Korean War and United States Economic Activity, 1950–1952*, National Bureau of Economic Research, Occasional Paper 49 (Princeton, 1955); and *Growth and Stability of the Postwar Economy*, Brookings Institution (Washington, 1960).

pointed the way to a widening of Hirst's views. He was convinced that 'whoever wins on the field, both sides lose in wealth'.[1] The size of the loss as far as Britain was concerned he put as between two and four years' normal accumulation of capital. He attributed the low level of employment in the 1920s to the scarcity of capital brought about by its destruction and depreciation in the war. The other long-term effects of the war which he was able to demonstrate proved the starting-point of much discussion. He agreed that the expenses of the war had resulted in a much greater burden of taxation, but demonstrated that the cumulative effect of this taxation was to redistribute a certain amount of income from the richer to the poorer. Taken together with the high level of employment during the war, the long hours and the high wages, and even when all allowance had been made for the wretched pittance paid to the soldiers, the net result was a narrowing of the gap between the poorer classes and the richer. Bowley also drew attention to other effects of the war, the great advances made in communications, the development of the internal combustion engine and, even more strikingly, of the aircraft industry which had scarcely existed in 1914, the advances in theoretical science and in engineering which war had stimulated, and the change in the economic relationship between Britain and the United States.

But it was his perception of the social change brought about by war which had the greatest effect. Not only had the war reduced the gap between the classes and even brought into existence a system of taxation the effect of whose operations would be to continue to reduce that gap, but its events, and the involvement of so large a part of the population in them, had changed the general outlook of society. They had provided a perception of another system. 'The economic position of women and their more complete enfranchisement and independence with its multiform consequence, would no doubt have developed in a different manner if their claims had not been substantiated by their ability to replace men. In a somewhat similar way the services of all ranks in the Army and Navy, and the more general intermixture of classes, stimulated the sentiment of democracy and led to a more serious realisation of possibly avoidable econ-

[1] A. L. Bowley, *Some Economic Consequences of the Great War* (1930) p. 31.

omic inequalities and hardships, thus paving the way for the development of the insurance schemes and of more socialistic legislation.'[1]

Bowley was surely right to suggest that war was also a force for change rather than a wholly negative and retrogressive event. But a force for change in which direction? Many involved in the administration of the economy during the First World War would have answered, a force for change towards a less wasteful capitalism. Such was the standpoint of one of the most influential accounts of the effects of the First World War, that of Edward Lloyd. Briefly, Lloyd's attitude might be characterised as one of regret that the experiments in economic administration undertaken during the war had been abandoned after 1918 and also as one of certainty that, despite their abandonment, they represented a long-term trend in the modification of liberal capitalism in Britain and thus that their abandonment would prove only temporary. The principal effect of the First World War was therefore, he argued, to accelerate a transformation in the economic system. 'Thirdly,' he wrote, 'I am disinclined to admit that *all* the measures of industrial and commercial organisation adopted during the war, which are commonly lumped together under the term state control, were merely necessary evils to be got rid of as soon as possible and never to be thought about again. A considerable extension of co-operative and collective enterprise seems to me probable and desirable in times of peace; and I believe that there is something to be learnt from the experiments in state control during the war which may be of positive value in the difficult times ahead. . . . When the time comes for computing the total net cost of the war and its after-effects, what little there is to be set down on the credit side will need to be sifted with microscopic care from the evil consequences which leap at once to the eye; and among these changes and developments that may appear to some to contain the germs of a better order of society a place may perhaps be found for some features, at any rate, of the experiments described in this volume.'[2]

Lloyd did not think that the First World War foreshadowed any fundamental change in the economic system, but that it foreshadowed the growth of larger firms organised in associations

[1] Ibid., p. 22.
[2] E. M. H. Lloyd, *Experiments in State Control* (1924) preface.

and trusts, of larger trade unions negotiating at a national rather than a local level, of the development of state control as a regulating force in the economy, of the elimination of the wastes which he attributed to the more intensely competitive system which had prevailed before 1914. The greater concentration of firms and the greater size of trade unions have been the results of so many converging trends in the twentieth-century economy that it is hardly possible to measure the part played by the war in these processes. The interest of his book and its subsequent influence did not only depend on his excellent account of the development of state interference in the economy but on the extent to which his forecasts appeared to have been fulfilled in the 1930s. He himself gloomily reflected that all that was left of the war economy were protectionist and nationalist tariffs 'and the economic clauses of a Treaty which threatened to destroy the possibility of stable reconstruction'.[1] But certain measures of control abandoned between 1918 and 1920 did indeed reappear in various disguises in the 1930s, agricultural price supports and certain tariff devices for example, and those that had not done so by 1939 were quickly reimposed when the Second World War broke out. 'Organised competition', Lloyd wrote, 'pits like with like, and measures their comparative efficiency with precision; the free play of the competitive system confers its rewards and punishments indiscriminately.' He would certainly have acknowledged the type of capitalism which developed in Britain after the Second World War as being the result, in part, of the First World War.

The rapid abandonment of state controls after 1918 was equally disappointing to those historians who believed that the pressure for social change built up by the war amounted to more than a mere desire to modify the type of capitalism in Britain. R. H. Tawney argued that the dismantling of economic controls was both inevitable and mistaken in so far as it was against the long-term historical trend. His summary of the effects of the war is almost exactly like that of Lloyd. 'The period of war economy accelerated the demise of the individualist, competitive phase of British capitalism. It stimulated organisation and combination among manufacturers; advertised rationalisation; strengthened the demand for tariffs; and encouraged, in another sphere, the

[1] E. M. H. Lloyd, *Experiments in State Control*, p. 371.

settlement of wages and working conditions by national rather than by local agreements.'[1] Tawney expressed his views cautiously, perhaps conscious that he was a specialist in another period, but more likely impressed by the speed with which the country had returned to 'normal'. There had been, he ruefully admitted, no 'intellectual conversion' to economic control.

But the gross failure of the return to 'normality' in the 1920s, the growth of collectivisation in the 1930s and the success of the economic controls applied in the Second World War cheered those of Tawney's outlook; it may be no coincidence that Tawney should have published his article in 1943. The Second World War was so much more 'total' even than the First World War that it reawakened interest in the work not only of Lloyd but also of Bowley. Under the pressure of war the same social changes that Bowley had identified earlier took place, and seemed related to the greater involvement of the population as a whole in the war.

In 1954 Andrzejewski published his theory of the 'military participation ratio'.[2] This was derived from the general idea, frequently discussed after 1914, and implied in Bowley's work, that there was some inherent connection between the extent to which war involved the total population and the extent of social change. Andrzejewski argued that the extent of social welfare in any society varied with the extensiveness of the social groups required to fight in its wars. There is always a gap between the actual military participation ratio, the proportion of those who take part to those that are not involved, and the optimum military participation ratio, the proportion that would allow society to fight its wars most effectively. The relevance of such a theory to the twentieth century is easy to see. Adam Smith believed that the maximum possible ratio of combatants to civilians was 1 in 100; Germany and France in the First World War mobilised 1 in 10. By measuring the gap between the actual and the optimum it would be possible to show which social groups would become involved in future wars and, more importantly, which social groups would therefore benefit by being able to make their claims on the state felt.

[1] R. H. Tawney, 'The Abolition of Economic Controls, 1918–1921', *Economic History Review*, XIII (1943).

[2] S. Andrzejewski, *Military Organisation and Society* (1954).

Titmuss, more cautiously, proposed roughly similar conclusions which he held to have been demonstrated by the changes in social policy during the Second World War. Less crude than Andrzejewski's theory, Titmuss's views are nevertheless closely related.[1] 'Total war' is a war of a total society. Previously social policy had been concerned with alleviating the lot of particular groups or classes, the unemployed, the widowed, the old, the orphaned and so on. Only some were involved in unemployment or widowhood; all were involved in war. The bomber did not discriminate. Against its menace the only remedy at first seemed to be to minimise the general panic which would ensue. In March 1939 the Ministry of Health had asked the India Office for the loan of an official used to dealing with large crowds, of the kind that might pour in panic from bombed London. By summer 1940, however, practical relief on the spot was provided for all. School meals were no longer only provided for the 'necessitous', issues of special welfare foods and vitamins were made to all. Old-age pensions were generally increased even in war, the hated household means test for social service payments was abolished. From 1942 onwards, in spite of the war, the general health of British society began to improve strikingly.[2] The implication of Titmuss's views is that the Welfare State as it came to exist in the late 1940s owed its existence by that date to the Second World War. It should not be forgotten that when Beveridge issued his more or less freelance report proposing a comprehensive social insurance system which would be obligatory for all citizens during the war, it became, for all its arid nature, a bestseller.[3] And the administrative foundations of the National Health Service were greatly strengthened by the need to organise a national hospital system for civilians during the war.

Andrzejewski's theory has proved too precise for most others to swallow. It was in particular criticised by Abrams.[4] Abrams considered the history of the ill-starred Ministry of Reconstruc-

[1] R. M. Titmuss, *Problems of Social Policy* (1950); and *Essays on the 'Welfare State'* (1958).

[2] Ministry of Health, *On the State of the Public Health during Six Years of War* (1946).

[3] Sir William Beveridge, *Social Insurance and Allied Services*, *Parliamentary Papers*, VI (1942–3).

[4] P. Abrams, 'The Failure of Social Reform, 1918–1920', *Past and Present*, no. 24 (1963).

tion, created in the First World War. The social aspirations of those caught up in the process of social change tended to crystallise around this Ministry, which in 1918 and 1919 issued a series of highly interesting reports outlining and advocating reforms in almost every aspect of administration and policy, but was eventually able to achieve nothing except its own disappearance in the depression. Certainly it must be admitted that the history of this Ministry is one of the neglected themes of British history, but Abrams's article, drawn as it is largely from the memoirs of the Minister himself, is scarcely profound enough to illuminate what happened to it. Abrams suggests that the only group which appears to have benefited in terms of Andrzejewski's hypothesis was middle-aged propertied women, to whom, of course, the franchise was extended. Other groups were unable to benefit from their involvement in the war because they were unable to force their wishes through a traditional administration. Furthermore the idea, felt by many social reformers, that there was a 'harmony of spirit' in the war led them to suppose that they had already, owing to the effects of the war, achieved their aims. 'In short, in its crude form the "military participation ratio" theory of social reform will not do. If it is to have any value, it must also allow for the fact that different groups in society participate in a war effort in different degree with widely varying power to influence consequential political decisions, and with a very different sense of what participation means to them. Thus in 1914–1918 participation in the war effort meant for some a loss of freedom of action and expression in the interests of national economic co-operation; for others it meant an entirely new and effective entry into the arenas of policy-making.' In other words, in Abrams's view, Titmuss takes rather too bland a view of social differences.

Marwick, however, rejects Abrams's criticisms while also finding the 'military participation ratio' theory too crude.[1] The general tendency of his work is to support the interpretation of Titmuss, while at the same time returning to the themes canvassed by Lloyd. Abrams, he argues, does not pay sufficient attention to the 'unguided social changes' which the world wars brought about.[2] The significant aspect of war is that it introduces

[1] A. Marwick, *Britain in the Century of Total War* (1968); and *The Deluge* (1965).

[2] *Britain in the Century of Total War*, p. 15.

an element of 'discontinuity' into a historical pattern of gradual-
ness and stability, thus tending both to introduce and to accelerate
social change. The mechanism by which these changes are
brought about is twofold. The climate of social consciousness
changes in the direction of greater homogeneity between social
classes, and this trend is reinforced by technological improvements. Developments in broadcasting and motor transport, for
example, starting in the First World War on a large scale, were
to draw society in the twenties and thirties more closely together.[1]
Marwick's position is thus to emphasise the importance of the
world wars in accelerating a number of social trends of which
Abrams has tended to play down the importance. His viewpoint
rests on more reading than Abrams's; neither, however, rests on
research.

Present interpretations have left Hirst a long way behind. His
lament over the increasing burden of public debt and over the
'colossal augmentation of the bureaucracy'[2] are now usually seen
as misplaced. Both the changes in financial policy and the growth
of the civil service are rather seen as significant symptoms of a
welcome social change.

The Domestic Impact

ONE thing may be remarked about the more recent interpretations – their parochiality. Were we to ask a citizen of Japan,
Russia or Germany whether he perceived an extraordinary degree
of change in our society over the period from 1914, and were he to
use his own society as a yardstick, he might well reply that he did
not. It has been fairly pointed out that the actual social reforms
which Titmuss can unequivocally attribute to war are neither
very numerous nor very impressive: the free treatment of
venereal disease, free immunisation against diphtheria, an
increase in the number of children provided with milk and
dinners at school and the abolition of the household means test,
which has in any case tended to creep back in disguises. To claim

[1] Ibid., pp. 125 ff.
[2] Hirst and Allen, *British War Budgets*, p. 16.

the Welfare State and the major changes in the British economy which it implied as the result of the war is to place a lot of strain on the concept of a change of social attitude during the war. Yet there can be no doubt that war did change social aspirations and that this change in its turn was connected with changes in the economic system. The question is, what changes? It is here that we must step outside the periphery of these theories of social change to examine the more empirical research of those who have pursued the paths first opened up by Bowley. How, precisely, did the economic and social system change as a result of the world wars?

Even more striking an aspect of the parochiality of the interpretations we have been considering is their assumption that the most important effects of the world wars on the British economy were attributable to changes that took place in Britain. It will be necessary to question that assumption later by looking at the impact on the British economy of changes caused elsewhere by the world wars, and to ask whether they are not at least as significant for Britain as the changes which took place in this country. For the moment, however, we must confine our attentions within the national frontiers.

Certain social and economic changes may clearly be singled out as a result of government action. An obvious one is the dramatic change in fortune which the Second World War brought to the agricultural sector of the economy. The effects of the German submarine blockade in the First World War were to lead the British Government in 1917, by the use of financial incentives and by compulsory powers which were hardly used, to attempt to reverse the trend of agricultural development in Britain over the previous forty years. That trend had been to a diminution of the labour force, an increase in grassland and in the production of some meats and of dairy foods, and a drastic decrease in other crops, particularly cereals. The attempt to reconvert to arable farming was relatively successful and the crop area in 1918 was greater by 3 million acres than in 1916. The various financial incentives were embodied in the Corn Production Act, 1917, which fixed minimum prices for wheat and oats. The Ministry of Reconstruction advocated the retention of these measures on the statute book in peacetime and the Agriculture Act, 1920, established a system of annual price reviews for farm produce. Less than one year later with the onset of the depression this Act was repealed and the previous trend of agricultural development reasserted itself. Before the Second World War the government's assumption was that it would be able to manage its economy while still retaining agricultural prices at their pre-war level. There were two reasons why this proved impossible: the increase in imported fodder prices and the powerful and successful pressure which farmers were able to bring to bear on the government in the new circumstances, pressure to which the government quite deliberately yielded.[1]

The occasion of their capitulation was the decision in June 1940 to lay down a minimum national wage for agricultural workers instead of minimum local wages, itself a reflection of the suddenly increased importance of agriculture. Faced with this extra increase in costs, which would have meant an extra annual wage bill for the industry of £15 million, farmers demanded a wide range of higher and guaranteed prices. The effect of their pressure, which was continued throughout the war, appears in an interesting book by Seers. Dividing the income-receivers into various groups and comparing the value of the *per capita* pre-tax income received by each group, he is able to demonstrate that the increase in farmers' incomes between 1938 and 1949 on an average was seven-and-a-half-fold.[2] Certain professional groups alone did better, but when allowance is made for taxation the improvement accruing to them was easily outdistanced by that accruing to farmers. By comparison the improvement accruing to wage-earners on an average *per capita* pre-tax basis was two-and-a-half-fold. Agricultural labourers, of course, did much less well than farmers.

There can be no doubt that not only did the farming community enormously improve its position in the economy as a result of the world wars, but that that improvement has been a long-term one. The system of guaranteed prices and annual price reviews, acting, as it were, as an insurance taken out by the state on behalf of the farmer against the risk of crop failure, has been maintained in full vigour since 1940. Although that system

[1] E. F. Nash, 'Wartime Control of Food and Agricultural Prices', in *Lessons of the British War Economy*, National Institute of Economic and Social Research (Cambridge, 1951).

[2] D. Seers, *Changes in the Cost of Living and the Distribution of Income since 1938* (Oxford, 1949).

did not long survive the First World War, the principles of the Agriculture Act, 1920, were gradually introduced in the 1930s and by 1945 seemed almost universally accepted.[1] If we turn, however, to other social groups in a position to benefit, the position is less obvious, partly because those groups are both more amorphous and often more divided amongst themselves than the farmers.

Bowley originally identified wage-earners as a group who benefited from the First World War, and subsequent writers have suggested that to them should be added those who lent money to the government. The two questions cannot be separated, for they are bound together by the highly inflationary method by which the government chose to finance the First World War. Inflation is a most powerful cause of social change, and in a period when what was produced by the economy, and the rewards distributed for producing it, were subject in themselves to drastic change, inflation could only increase the sense of a changing order.

The causes of the inflation in the First World War have received sufficient attention to merit a further pamphlet. Simplifying drastically, it could be said that the impact of the war on the international economy was inflationary and that this was exacerbated by domestic financial policy. The demand from all the powers involved for raw materials and finished products was so great as to cause a general rise in the price of imports which in turn caused British wholesale prices to move upwards sharply in the spring of 1915. International demand was sustained on this level throughout the war, but its impact on Britain was probably less important than the government's own constantly increasing demands on the domestic economy. The government was able to satisfy this demand by borrowing on a massive scale, until 1917 in the form of three separate long-term loans and after that date more by short- and medium-term borrowing. All the forms of paper which the government issued to finance the gap between expenditure and revenue from taxation were in themselves sources of credit. The deficit thus provided for a general increase in purchasing power, although there must be a strong presumption, since the degree of inflation in Britain was less than in

[1] The political circumstances in which the Agriculture Act, 1920, was repealed would certainly repay further investigation.

many other countries, that government financial policy permitted the inflation to occur rather than caused it.[1]

The effect of the 'war economy' organised between 1914 and 1918 was to transfer real resources to the government from the private economy, but the 'McKenna rule' meant that this transfer was not accompanied by any really adequate restrictions on private purchasing power. The spectacle of luxury spending by a small number during the war sharpened the edge of social and economic criticism. To ensure an adequate supply of funds, the interest rate on money had to be increased repeatedly, only falling after 1917 when certain economic controls became really effective. Those who lent to the government were therefore able to protect themselves against inflation, while at the same time the government provided them with important concessions in the payment of death duties and, after the war, while reducing the mounting burden of debt, offered them relatively favourable terms of conversion.

Hirst, while lamenting the increase in government debt, believed that this process had had one obviously beneficial effect, a wider distribution of capital. Not only were people who had not been accustomed to invest attracted into the investment market by the flood of government paper on favourable terms, but many workers, particularly those in munitions factories, were able to accumulate a considerable fund of savings for the first time in their lives. There was of course a distinct probability that this would be the result of an economy where production for civilian purposes was increasingly restricted and where foodstuffs were increasingly scarce whereas earnings appeared to be much higher. The same ideas lay behind Keynes's now celebrated articles, *How to Pay for the War*, which appeared in *The Times* in 1940[2] where he pressed for a system of compulsory savings whereby the increased incomes accruing in the course of the war would be temporarily withheld until after the war. The result would be that the government would be able to borrow more easily during the war and without such apparent social injustice, and after the war, by releasing the extra income, would be able to

[1] E. V. Morgan, *Studies in British Financial Policy, 1914–25* (1952); F. McVey, *The Financial History of Great Britain, 1914–1918* (New York, 1918); A. W. Kirkaldy (ed.), *British Finance, during and after the War, 1914–21* (1921).

[2] J. M. Keynes, *How to Pay for the War* (1940).

combat the post-war depression by increasing purchasing power. The working classes would thus liquidate their claims on goods when goods were available instead of liquidating them to the embarrassment of the government. The payment would be made from the results of a capital levy. Wage-earners would be made to reduce some of the inequalities of the capitalist system instead of merely indulging in pleasure. Keynes, who had been much influenced by the social changes of the First World War, saw in the Second World War a most excellent opportunity to further such changes.

His ideas were only in part accepted by the government, and in that part wherein they were anti-inflationary.[1] For fear of another inflation of the same kind had long been the mainspring of Treasury policy. The abandonment of the gold exchange standard in the 1930s and the acceptance of exchange controls, making the impact of international monetary movements much less direct, enabled the government to maintain the interest rate on government long-term borrowing at 3 per cent throughout the Second World War. More importantly the whole-hearted acceptance that it was necessary to impose a battery of restrictions and physical controls on the civilian economy and to increase taxation from the outset, meant that the more glaring social inequalities of the First World War were avoided. But the same demand for labour and the same increase in money wages existed even if financial policy was different; the underlying pressure towards social change was still there.

There is some evidence that Hirst was correct in his supposition that capital became more widely distributed. The War Savings Certificates issued in 1916 were originally intended to be issued only to those who had satisfied a means test, but the government abandoned that test as unnecessary. The number of small savers did increase, as witnessed by the continuation and success of the National Savings Movement after the Second World War. But these facts have to be seen in proportion. The War Wealth Committee calculated that 68 per cent of the total increase in wealth during the First World War went to that class which already possessed fortunes of more than £5,000, thus suggesting that the previous inequalities may have been intensified. There

[1] R. S. Sayers, *Financial Policy, 1939–45* (1956) gives an account of the development of opinion in the government independently of Keynes's ideas.

is a more careful check on these calculations in the work of E. V. Morgan. Before 1914 government securities in private hands were about $2\frac{1}{2}$ per cent of total private property; in the 1920s they had risen to almost 25 per cent. The main owners of all this government paper, however, were extra-budgetary funds, like the National Health Insurance Fund, banks and firms in the money market. Between 1914 and 1919 small savers absorbed about £487 million of the National Debt, and between then and 1924 a further £131 million. The total debt was £6,592 million.[1] In the tax year 1924–5, £67,923,000 of securities changed hands on the death of their owners; only £1,385,000 were in estates to the value of less than £100. Nevertheless it should also be said that the proportion of securities to the total size of estate was greater in the smaller estates.

Rough measurements of the holdings of capital show that there has been a tendency to redistribution in this century but that that tendency has been very slight. The percentage of the national stock of capital owned by those owning between £1,000 and £5,000 was just under 16 per cent in the period 1911–13; in the period 1924–30 it was about $17\frac{1}{2}$ per cent. There was little change between that date and 1936–8, but between 1946 and 1947 the percentage was about $21\frac{1}{2}$ per cent. That proportion of the national stock held by those holding less than £1,000, however, increased only very slightly, whereas that proportion held by those holding over £100,000 fell most markedly.[2] There is thus considerable evidence in favour of a redistribution of capital accelerated by the world wars, but little evidence that this touched the poorest groups. Looking outside the boundaries of Britain again, it is impossible not to be more impressed by the stability of the pattern of capital holding in Britain when compared, for example, to Germany, where capital holdings have twice been almost wiped out. In 1911–13, 1 per cent of the persons aged over twenty-five in England and Wales owned 70 per cent of the total capital; in 1946–7, 1 per cent owned 50 per cent of the total. Little is known of the level of working-class savings in the First World War, but studies at the close of the Second World War suggest that there were great inequali

[1] Morgan, *Studies in British Financial Policy*, pp. 122 ff.

[2] K. Langley, 'The Distribution of Capital in Private Hands 1936–8 and 1946–7', *Bulletin of the Oxford University Institute Statistics*, XIII (1951).

according to the level of income. The poorer 52 per cent of a sample of working-class families studied by Durant and Goldmann in 1944–5 owned only 9 per cent of the aggregate savings total of the sample, while at the other end of the scale 12 per cent of the families owned 50 per cent of the total savings.[1] In general the remarkable thing about the level of working-class savings is how low it was.

So low was the level of soldiers' pay that it is reasonable to suppose that if the wars did provide a boost to the working-class standard of living, the rewards must have been distributed arbitrarily according to the occupation of the head of the family. Bowley noted that the demand for labour between 1914 and 1918 did leave some permanent effect. In 1911, 703,000 females were gainfully employed in the clothing trade; in 1921 only 503,000 were so employed.[2] But the total number of females in gainful employment increased by 234,000 in the same period. The increase is accounted for by the greater number of female workers remaining in employment in the metal industries and in the engineering and shipbuilding industries. In the latter category only 8,000 females were employed in 1911 and 42,000 in 1921. The biggest increase in female employment over that period was in the civil service, from 33,000 to 102,000. It may be argued that Bowley's conclusions require modification, for after 1921 in the course of the depression there was a great deal of replacement of female labour by male labour. Since the categories of the standard industrial classification as used in the Census Reports changed in that year, it is difficult to extrapolate Bowley's calculations with any accuracy after 1921. Nevertheless some traditionally male jobs, shop assistant and civil servant, for example, did not remain so sexually exclusive after 1918. There is a good deal of circumstantial evidence to indicate that the level of female employment in the 1920s was higher than a mere continuation of the pre-1914 trend after 1921 would indicate. It is certainly true that the level of female employment in the 1950s was higher than a mere extrapolation of the trend before 1939.

In the Second World War, in June 1943, the highest number of registered unemployed was 112,000 persons only. There were

[1] H. Durant and J. Goldmann, 'The Distribution of Working-Class Savings', *Bulletin of the Oxford University Institute of Statistics*, VII (1945).

[2] Bowley, *Some Economic Consequences of the Great War*, p. 171.

4,745,000 men and women in the armed forces and their auxiliary services.[1] Since there was little unemployment after 1945, the Second World War achieved what the First World War may not have permanently achieved and brought a large number of women into the fully-employed labour force. Taking a category of employment where the census classifications did not change too drastically, that of transport and communications, the number of women employed was in 1901, 27,000, in 1911, 38,000, in 1921, between 72,000 and 75,000 depending on the classification used, in 1931, 82,000, and in 1951, 149,000. After 1921 a special classification to indicate clerks and typists was introduced, although it was not always observed in the same manner. The number of women employed in public administration and in commercial occupations increased from 105,000 in 1901, to 207,000 in 1911 and to 668,000 in 1921 by the old classification. Using the new classification and combining the categories of public administration, commercial, financial and insurance occupations, and clerks and typists in order to smooth out certain vagaries of allocation, the number of women so employed was 1,149,000 in 1921, 1,152,000 in 1931 and 2,286,000 in 1951.

In both wars hours of work were long. Yet it cannot be simply assumed that the impact of the demand for labour was to put up the real wages and the standard of living of the largest section of the community. The extent of rationing and other economic controls, together with increasing taxation and rising prices, makes the actual level of real wages and the wider issue of the standard of living difficult to determine. In addition, as several interesting studies have shown, demand for labour was very complex in its incidence.

The level of real wages in both wars has usually been measured by the retail prices collected by employment exchanges from 1914 onwards, which later became the Board of Trade cost-of-living index. On this basis it appears that only in the last year of the First World War was there a general substantial gain in real wage rates as opposed to money wages, although it must be remembered that because of overtime pay earnings were often much higher

[1] Sir G. Ince, 'The Mobilisation of Manpower in Great Britain for the Second World War', *Manchester School of Social and Economic Studies*, XIV (1946).

than before 1914.[1] Bowley distinguished sharply between the fortunes of the unskilled workers and those of the skilled artisans. Statistical investigations in five English towns made in 1912–14 and 1923–4 revealed that whereas in 1913 a considerable number of workers, although in full-time employment, did not earn a sufficient wage to keep them out of poverty, this had become very rare by 1924. Bowley attributed this mainly to the demand for labour during the war forcing up the wage rates of the lowest paid. 'The skilled artisan', he wrote, 'had gained little by 1924, except the reduction of working hours.'[2]

Concluding his chapter on changes in income distribution, Bowley drew attention to three trends in particular: the tendency to eliminate 'remediable poverty', the tendency to diminish 'excessive wealth', and the tendency to a more equal distribution of incomes. 'The changes are due to many factors, some of which are directly traceable to the war, while others, such as the fall of the birth-rate and the extension of social services, are the continuation of processes that began before the war, which, however, cannot have been without influence on the manner and date of their development.'[3] Wise words, but Bowley made little of one force which has since received much attention, which was certainly present during the First and Second World Wars, and which operated in such a way as to cause a permanent change in the structure of jobs within the factory and thus in the structure of the wage pattern. This force was the tendency of certain industries to move to a much higher level of productivity than in peacetime.

The origins of this drive towards productivity lay in the need to produce relatively standardised but often extremely complex goods in huge numbers. Nearly a quarter of a million ·303-in. machine-guns were manufactured in the First World War, all more or less to a pattern; 849,923 were made in the Second World War. Almost 4 million rifles were turned out in the First World War.[4] The tank, not really used in battle until 1917, had by 1918 become a mass-produced good. The aeroplane, still an object of

---

[1] A. L. Bowley, *Prices and Wages in the United Kingdom, 1914–20* (1921).

[2] Bowley, *Some Economic Consequences of the Great War*, p. 160.

[3] Ibid., p. 165.

[4] W. C. Hornby, *Factories and Plant* (1958) p. 10.

curiosity in 1914, had also entered into the stage of mass-production by 1917. The size of the British aircraft industry in 1918 is often forgotten. 52,027 military aeroplanes were manufactured in the First World War, not much less than half the total manufactured between 1939 and 1944, although of course the earlier machines were simpler. The development of production on such a scale led to new methods of doing old jobs, new methods of factory layout, new methods of management and more intensive mechanisation.

Not only did the First World War produce the first thoroughly consistent application of work study to solve the new problems of mass-production, but it greatly changed the equipment with which people produced. The massive scale of government orders and the urgency to fulfil them led at the start of the war to a great increase in the installation of machine-tools, particularly turret lathes, capstan lathes and universal milling machines, many of which had to be imported from the United States where the general level of mechanisation within the factory was much higher. As the level of orders grew, and as the conscription of the semi-skilled men who operated such machines grew also, the tendency to install automatic machine-tools which could be used by quite unskilled labour developed. At the same time older machines were adapted to use by unskilled labour. Not only was there a great increase in the use of machine-tools but also a great improvement in their deployment, especially after the government census of machine-tools in 1915. The gun, aeroplane and tank factories of 1918, in their equipment and layout and in their methods of organisation, bore little resemblance to most British factories of 1913.

It could be argued that in fact output per man declined in Britain in the Second World War, although the same tendencies operated as in the First World War. But the problem is to consider the long-term and not the short-term effects of war. The difficulties in securing regular delivery, the lack of investment, the tendency to overuse fixed capital, the inferior nature of some of the materials used and the substitution of older men and females for those conscripted into the armed forces all tend to reduce the level of productivity at the time. The First World War led to a growth in output in a number of industries in which the significant improvements in productivity seemed to have been made long before and where there now appeared only restricted possibilities of technological advance.[1] Such was the case with the shipbuilding industry. Expansion there, and in coal-mining, has often been blamed for the so-called 'excess capacity' of the 1920s and the subsequent depression. Nevertheless it might be observed that before 1939 in the United States it took thirty-five weeks to produce a standard warship, whereas in 1943 it took fifty days.[2]

In the long run it is the innovatory aspect of war which impresses more than its temporary restrictive aspects. When relatively new industries were expanded by the guaranteed markets of wartime, they showed astonishing increases in productivity. The cost of manufacturing a long-range bomber in the United States in 1940 was $15.18 per hour; in 1944 it was $4.82. The industrial sectors which were in expansion during the wars were often more capital-intensive than those whose output was restricted. Many were completely new industries of great importance for the future, for the pressure of both wars brought a remarkable increase in the rate of scientific and technological discovery. The development of radio receivers, of nuclear fission, of radar, of better tractors, of the jet engine, of new alloys, of optical glass, of measuring tools, of synthetic materials, of electronic computing and control systems and of a wide range of therapeutic drugs were all due largely to research for military purposes, and the list could be much extended. It was no coincidence that the Department of Scientific and Industrial Research came into existence during the First World War.

It might be asked whether there was any significant difference in this respect in the two world wars, for the tendency in historical argument has often been to blame the effect of industrial expansion in 1914–18 for the aftermath of that war and to take almost the opposite line when dealing with the Second World War. In this respect also the effect on long-run productivity of the Utility Scheme, which standardised many consumer goods in the Second World War, might also be examined. So might the tendency for government contracts to be allocated to larger firms while smaller firms are closed down for lack of raw materials.[3] All that can be

[1] W. H. B. Court, *Coal* (1951) is a first-rate study of a similar problem of declining productivity in the Second World War.

[2] P. Grand'Jean, *Guerres, Fluctuations et Croissance* (Paris, 1967).

[3] There is an account of government 'concentration' policy in G. C. Allen, 'The Concentration of Production Policy', in N.I.E.S.R., *Lessons of the British War Economy* (1951).

said at this stage is that there is scope for more research on these questions before any pronouncement which is not merely theoretical can be made.

About the effects of this greater level of mechanisation on the work force, however, it is possible to be more precise. That contracts for the supply of the armed forces at the outset of war required an immediate increase in skilled labour such as to produce an acute shortage of such workers appears to have been a universal phenomenon in both wars.[1] The national response was to increase the level of standardisation and mechanisation so as to reduce this need. In the very first stages of the First World War there was also an increase in the number of those employed in unskilled jobs. Meanwhile women replaced men in clerical work and in retail trade. As mechanisation proceeded, the need for semi-skilled workers to operate the new machines increased more rapidly than the need for skilled workers.[2] It was this that caused the first 'dilution' agreements of 1915, for the job pattern was changed by taking away from the skilled artisan the more mechanical parts of his job and having them performed on the new machines by the semi-skilled. Since most wages were paid by piece-rates, or had similar incentive bonuses attached, the skilled worker's income was reduced relative to that of the semi-skilled worker. After the conclusion of the Shells and Fuses Agreement in March 1915 the manufacturers began to install large numbers of automatic machines, which had made their first appearance in boot factories and now began to transform shell factories. With their appearance came the final stage of the concept of the mechanised production line, to spread rapidly from shell factories into many other manufactures. These machines needed only unskilled labour and it was with their installation that women first moved into factory jobs in significant numbers. The Dilution Scheme worked out in October 1915 finally consigned the skilled artisan to the tool-room and saw the replacement of semi-skilled workers by unskilled workers and women. This replacement was accompanied by constant improvements in

[1] See, for example, A. F. Hinrichs, 'The Defence Program and Labor Supply in the United States', *Canadian Journal of Economics and Political Science*, VII (1941).

[2] G. D. H. Cole, *Trade Unionism and Munitions* (1923); I. O. Andrews, *Economic Effects of the War upon Women and Children in Great Britain* (New York, 1918).

the earnings of the unskilled, whose whole function in the factory had been changed by this rapid mechanisation. By 1917 women were performing in many industries jobs which in a different form had been performed by semi-skilled male workers before the war and by the close of the war some were classed as skilled. This substitution of labour was less difficult than had been imagined, for as the nature of the job changed so did the need for training diminish and the category of 'semi-skilled' lost its former meaning. In fact the pattern of the employment of women in the First World War is most instructive. They became a new industrial proletariat, but the position and income of that proletariat had been drastically altered by the war.

Bowley's statistical observations are thus confirmed from other directions. It is curious that they have received so little attention from those historians for whom his work has been in other ways so suggestive a starting-point. The older statistical surveys of poverty in the manner of Booth and Rowntree show that it was all too possible for men to be in full employment before 1914 and to be dying of malnutrition through poverty, but for those in casual or spasmodic employment this wretched state was normal. All statistical surveys also agree that this was becoming unusual in the 1920s, although the general demand for labour was much slacker. Nor does it seem that the inadequately employed and rewarded before 1914 are quite the same as the unemployed of the 1920s. Here again it is only possible to point to the need for further research. Could the war really have had so dramatic an effect on the labour market as to change radically a pattern of employment apparently so long established in Britain? It may even be that the observed improvement in the manners and clothes of the working classes over this brief period, which so pleased many observers, was not so much due to the drop in their consumption of alcohol as has been suggested.[1]

Something may be said of the effect of the Second World War on wage-earners from the studies of Seers.[2] That part of the National Income embraced in the category of wages, forces' pay and social income increased by some £900 million at 1947 prices between 1938 and 1947. The gain was mainly attributable to

[1] By, among many, Marwick, *The Deluge*, p. 329; or Sir A. Newsholme, *Fifty Years in Public Health* (1935) p. 408.

[2] Seers, *Changes in the Cost of Living and the Distribution of Income since 1938.*

redistribution of income, especially from salary-earners and from net property income. Working-class income in 1947 was 59 per cent of private income, whereas in 1938 it was 55 per cent. The total real net income of the category that Seers identified as working-class rose by over 9 per cent, and of that category which he identified as middle-class it fell by more than 7 per cent. If, however, these calculations are made on a pre-tax rather than a post-tax basis, the gain appears as relatively insignificant. It then appears that the greater equality is due more to changes in the taxation system, including the institution of food subsidies, than it appears to have been in the First World War. Taxation had also become more progressive between 1914 and 1918, but to a much smaller degree, such that its most marked effect, rather than to improve the position of those with the lowest earnings, had been to reduce the number of very large incomes. From the figures in the report of the Colwyn Committee it would appear that the principal gainers from this redistribution were those whose incomes were between £200 and £1,000 a year.[1] The incidence of income and supertax combined reduced the highest incomes by one-twelfth in 1914 and by almost one-half in 1925. The number of people with gross incomes above £3,000 in 1913–1914 was 32,500, but that number above an equivalent income limit, allowing for the change in prices by 1924–5, was 24,000.[2] It would appear therefore that the most important force making for an improvement in the working-class position in the Second World War was the increase and greater progressiveness of taxation, and this must be attributed in large part to the need to pay for war.

That this improvement was the result of the war more than of the long-run development of the economy appears likely, for it was not inherent in the economic system but dependent on certain incidences of policy. These incidences were dictated entirely by the exigency of the situation. The Inland Revenue criticised Keynes's ideas in 1942, remarking that 'the purpose of the income tax is not the redistribution of income', and in February 1941 Churchill raised violent objections to an increase in the income tax on the grounds that taxation of the middle and

---

[1] *Report of the Committee on National Debt and Taxation, Parliamentary Papers*, 1927, XI.

[2] Bowley, *Some Economic Consequences of the Great War*, p. 138.

upper classes could go no further.[1] The improvement also depended on government policy in respect of foodstuffs and rent. The old-fashioned and inadequate Board of Trade cost-of-living index which measured prices on the level of basic working-class consumption, that is to say of the consumption of those who lived on little more than the minimum standard necessary for existence, was carefully stabilised, when it showed a tendency to rise too rapidly at the start of the war, by the use of food subsidies and rent control. It therefore ceased to measure the true cost of living as it came to have even less resemblance to working-class consumption than it had had before. Higher incomes meant that there was a greater consumption of alcohol, tobacco and amusements, the prices of which, not being included in the index, were not stabilised and therefore higher.[2] It is thus very hard to be precise about the movement of real wages during the Second World War. But they do not appear to have played so important a role as price control and taxation. 'The total effect of income tax and price changes up to 1948 was to transfer about £500 million at 1938 prices, some £1,000 million at today's prices [1948], of purchasing power from one-sixth of the United Kingdom to the remainder, cutting the real value of the purchasing power in the hands of the top sixth by some 30 per cent, and increasing the purchasing power in the hands of the remainder by about 25 per cent.'[3] A general fall in real wage rates in 1947 marked the beginning of the end of this process, since carried further by the gradual elimination of food subsidies and rent controls. The long-run tendency to a redistribution of income in the twentieth century has been very greatly accelerated by the two wars; indeed a very considerable part of that redistribution, although a long-term effect, may have been limited in its occurrence to the period of the two world wars themselves.

To sum up, there is considerable evidence to support the general arguments of Titmuss and Andrzejewski. Certain groups

[1] Sayers, *Financial Policy, 1939–45*, p. 78.

[2] W. K. Hancock and M. M. Gowing, *The British War Economy* (1949) p. 500. For the greater upward movement in real earnings than real wages, see J. L. Nicholson, 'Employment and National Income during the War', in *Bulletin of the Oxford University Institute of Statistics*, VII (1945).

[3] Seers, *Changes in the Cost of Living and the Distribution of Income since 1938.*

whose services became much more important in war were able to use this opportunity to improve their position more rapidly than it had been improving in peacetime and to retain their advantages in the long run after the wars. There remains the issue at stake between Abrams and Marwick as to the extent to which this social change was 'unguided'.

Two things stand out – that the wars did stimulate economic and social change and that that change was not very great, especially when the impact of the wars on other countries is considered. Sociological research on the impact of disasters on industrialised societies is instructive in this context. Sorokin, whose work was the starting-point for much subsequent research, considered that disaster, of which war might be considered one example, afforded a particularly favourable ground 'for the emergence of radically different social forms'.[1] This view has since tended to be modified according to the level of society at which the disaster strikes. Form and Loomis in particular have drawn attention to the prevalence of a concept of 'return to normalcy'.[2] So long as there is hope for the future, society will hope that that future will resemble the form of the society which is threatened by disaster. The significance of this heightened sense of the need to recover social equilibrium and to go back to 'normalcy' for the events of the 1920s and the return to the gold standard needs little indication here, the economic literature of the time being shot through with such concepts. It may also help to explain the extent to which the development of the British economy along the lines indicated by Lloyd in his study of the First World War has been accelerated by warfare on such a scale.

For it would surely be an exaggeration to suggest that the wars produced any profound change in the British economic system in spite of the strong pressure for change. The Local Armaments Committees which sprang up at the beginning of 1915 raised the spectre of workers' control to the extent that employers refused in many places to allow them to function. The attitude of the employers was bolstered by the Munitions of War Act of

[1] P. A. Sorokin, *Man and Society in Calamity* (New York, 1942) p. 120.

[2] W. H. Form and C. P. Loomis, 'The Persistence and Emergence of Social and Cultural Systems in Disasters', *American Sociological Review*, xxi (1956); W. H. Form, C. P. Loomis and S. Nosow, *Community in Disaster* (New York, 1958).

that year which even went so far as temporarily to impose a pass-book system on munitions workers whereby they were unable to secure future employment without a report from their previous employer. The revolt of 'Red Clydeside' is certainly one of many evidences that writers such as Titmuss and Marwick do tend, as Abrams suggests, to exaggerate the extent of social unity produced by the wars. Those imprisoned and deported without trial in those events could certainly be forgiven for thinking so. Further evidence lies in the growing tax evasion during the Second World War. It was during, not after, that war that the practice of rearranging financial affairs so as to pay as little as possible of the tax burden developed on a large scale. But there is much to suggest that the revolt on Clydeside was a revolt of the defeated; the workers' control movement had already been nipped in the bud.[1]

The events of both wars delivered a great impetus to the general trend within the economy, which was to a more rational, a more efficient and, above all, a more managed deployment of resources. Except in that direction there was a general reluctance of the government to intervene, but in that particular direction the need to win the war finally overcame reluctance. That the government should seize the opportunity of war to promote changes which it might consider desirable rather than necessary was an idea which remained unaccepted, as witnessed by the fate of Keynes's recommendations on deferred pay. At the start of the First World War the state rejected the idea of nationalising the armament firms, and the take-over of the railway companies, which foreshadowed their later reorganisation and nationalisation, was based on merely military considerations. The railway rolling stock remained the property of its private owners. In general the boards and associations which developed with the extension of physical controls were essentially compromises with private interests, both sides driven to compromise by the desperateness of the situation. Either the methods and functions of private business were grafted on to a government department, or a group of private firms became temporarily a branch of the public service, as in the case of the United Kingdom Oilseed Brokers' Association. The differences in method of operation were

[1] Historians have tended to neglect this topic. The best work is B. Pribicevic, *The Shop Stewards' Movement and Workers' Control, 1910–1922* (Oxford, 1959).

mostly to be explained by market factors. Even where the government 'took possession', as in the case of coal mines or flour mills, the phrase did not imply any effective change of ownership. The government accepted financial responsibility for the results of control and enjoyed the use of the plant for its own ends. As in the First World War so in the Second, most controls were resorted to only when unavoidable. Rent control had its origins in a rent strike. In both wars the idea of a capital levy was rejected.

Within these limitations, however, there can be no doubting the general economic effect of both wars. Their influence was not merely to produce the nationalisation of basic industries after 1945 but also to determine that that nationalisation would be dictated primarily by considerations of the optimum deployment of resources rather than by more radical social aims. The same is true for the reorganisation of the railways and the electricity supply industry in the 1920s. In October 1940 the Central Statistical Office of the War Cabinet Office made the first official systematic survey of National Income data. From that time onwards economic policy was increasingly decided on a basis of National Income accounting. In the same year income tax became more widely payable at source, the beginnings of the PAYE scheme. The tendency for firms, banks and trade unions to amalgamate was accelerated by both wars, just as the First World War produced collective bargaining for wages on a national rather than a local scale. Above all the Second World War produced the White Paper on full employment policy.

The comprehensive measures which Beveridge had proposed for social insurance, many of which were adopted after 1945, had implied that a state of relatively full employment was necessary for their success. Beveridge and the government moved towards the same goal, and the government White Paper on employment policy in May 1944[1] was the beginning of a deliberate and successful attempt to preserve full employment which was to last for over twenty years. Again the point at issue was the optimum utilisation of all resources to bolster a capitalism which had sometimes seemed in danger of collapsing in the inter-war period. It may be said, however, that the war once again demonstrated what was possible in this regard.

[1] *Employment Policy, Parliamentary Papers*, 1943–4, VIII.

The closer connection between science and industry which the First World War achieved strengthened this movement towards better management of resources, especially as it was itself encouraged by the miscellaneous collection of scholars, writers and reformers who had for long criticised the British economy and British society for their 'inefficiency'. The Haldane Committee appointed in August 1914 first moved the government along the road to the subsidisation of certain industries of particular strategic importance. Such industries were later singled out for protection in Britain's first breach with free trade, the McKenna tariff. The Privy Council Committee for Scientific and Industrial Research in their report for 1915–16 made no bones about their views on 'the economic problem'. 'There is already a certain number of large firms in this country who, realising the unity of interest between employers and employed, have systematically striven to raise the standard of living among their workers and to give them a direct interest in the firm's success. Some of these efforts have not been philanthropic; and where they have been so in intention they have been proved by experience not to require any such spur. But the small firm finds it as difficult to provide pensions or clubs as to pay for research laboratories or original workers. We believe that some form of combination for both purposes may be found to be essential if the smaller under-takings of this country are to compete effectively with the great trusts and combines of Germany and America.'[1]

The question might even be raised whether this tendency to better management of resources did not have as strong an effect on bringing about the reforms in public health, including the institution of the National Health Service, as the social pressure from below. Describing the fragmentary nature of provision for social services in 1918, the Ministry of Reconstruction Committee on these questions wrote, 'It must not be imagined that the anomalies there discussed are but infractions of some academic ideals of logical order, or are to be condemned as merely falling short of abstract canons of constitutional or administrative theory. The truth is that they touch the people very gravely, and that both individually and collectively the nation suffers through the

[1] *Report of the Committee of the Privy Council for Scientific and Industrial Research for the Year 1915–16*, p. 42, *Parliamentary Papers*, 1916, VIII.

cross-purposes and lack of system which permeate this huge corpus of ill-organised public effort.'[1] Their proposals were to reconstruct local administration in such a way that an approach to a more genuinely national system of medicine could be created. The medical profession were to be turned into an 'organised army'. Although the wars influenced thinking on public health by making it appear a more urgent problem, they urged it in directions in which it had already been guided, and it ought to be wondered whether the National Health Service did not eventually owe as much to the Webbs as to the wars.

Until further research into what is, after all, very recent history, the question must remain undecided. How far were social and economic changes, not in consonance with peacetime trends, brought about by war? How far were these economic and social changes which were not managed or were 'unguided'? How far were the changes that did take place the product of social pressure from below caused by the war, and how far were they merely the result of a drive towards a better deployment of resources?

The International Impact

THAT resources could not be squandered with the same profligacy as in the nineteenth century was a lesson driven home by the international effects of the world wars. The greater readiness to impose controls on the domestic economy in the Second World War reflected as much as anything else the greatly changed position of Britain in the international economy. It was no longer possible to feel so confident about obtaining supply. The Royal Commission on the Supply of Food and Raw Materials in Time of War, reporting in 1905, opined that with enough money and enough ships there would be no danger.[2] That there should not be enough money struck them as the more remote of those two possibilities. The first six months of the First World War confirmed their confidence. From the spring of 1915 onwards,

---

[1] Ministry of Reconstruction Pamphlets, no. 23.

[2] *Parliamentary Papers*, 1905, xxxix.

however, the visible signs of Britain's deteriorating situation in the international economy became constantly more apparent. The scaffolding of multilateral settlements, which before 1914 held together the structure of international trade, rested on two chief bases. The first was that of India's balance of payments deficit to Britain and the surpluses with other countries with which this deficit was financed, the second the trading balances between Britain, Europe and North America. The framework of settlements so gradually constructed was violently disrupted by the First World War, and the Second World War completed its destruction.

The financial crisis which occurred at the declaration of war in 1914 was in no sense a crisis of lack of confidence in sterling. It was due to the certain knowledge that the mechanism of international settlements and the pattern of international trade would inevitably be disrupted. It was easily allayed by the government's first acts of intervention in the economy which were to place their credit behind approved commercial bills payable by enemy and other debtors who were unable to meet their liabilities and to provide additional cover for shipping-insurance firms. The intention was that London's position at the centre of international trade and investment should not suffer in any way. For it was not until 1917 that submarine warfare caused the government to interfere drastically with civilian supply from overseas, and throughout the First World War there was a small flow of foreign investment from Britain, a situation of ease almost unimaginable to the Cabinets of 1939–45.

Between August and November 1914 the movement of sterling was towards London, and the Bank of England's gold reserve increased almost threefold in that period. But as the demand for armaments, machines and raw materials mounted to heights which even in 1915 were far greater than the Royal Commission of 1905 had supposed, so did the financial relationship between Britain and the United States change. The United States was the sole possible source of supply for much of the machinery needed, and her volume of exports to Britain increased to such an extent that the exchange rate of the pound to the dollar began to deteriorate in September 1915. What was happening was the beginning of the reversal of the roles of Britain and the United States, for heavy British investment in the United States in the nineteenth century had meant that for the period when the gold standard was in operation the United States had been the debtor and Britain the creditor.

The Chancellor of the Exchequer had given his opinion in 1914 that Britain could pay for five years of war merely from the proceeds of her foreign investments. In October 1915 the Anglo-French Commission had to raise a loan of $500 million in the United States to finance the purchase of war supplies, in spite of the sale of securities and controlled payment by bullion. After the United States' entry into the war restrictions on lending to Britain almost disappeared. Indeed it is fortunate for Britain's sake that they did so. 'At the very moment that the United States came into the war, the British Government, with commitments in the United States running into hundreds of millions of pounds, was at the end of its tether. It had no means whatever of meeting them. Between that date and the Armistice it borrowed from the American Government to pay for "absolute necessities of life and warfare" not far short of £1,000 million.'[1] At the end of the war, therefore, Britain, besides being a general short-term debtor to the extent of £800 million, had also become a long-term debtor to the U.S.A. The so-called 'war debt' itself amounted to over £1,150 million.

It was not a contraction in the gold reserve which meant that London was never able to recover its pre-war position in international trade. In general that reserve was much higher in the 1920s than it had been before 1914. But the strength of London's position had always been the fact that Britain was a creditor on so vast a scale. It had only been necessary to cause some slackening in the rate of short-term lending in order to bring gold flowing back into London in payment of bills. After 1918 this happy position had disappeared. The exchange rate of the pound sterling was always likely to be worsened by the fact that much of the foreign money in London, being in short-term balances, could be and was withdrawn fairly quickly. The abandonment of the gold standard and the variety of devices used to replace it in the 1930s did not solve these problems, and in the years immediately before the Second World War Britain developed a deficit on balance of payments. The consequences of Britain's international indebtedness were much more far-reaching than those of the domestic indebtedness which Hirst bemoaned.

[1] Brand, *War and National Finance*, p. ix.

The process begun during the First World War was to be completed during the Second World War. Controls on trade were imposed almost from the start, so that except for a brief period when exports to dollar countries received high priority, the general level of exports dropped very sharply. British exports to India dropped from £34 million in 1938 to £18 million in 1943. Therefore Britain paid for overseas supply more and more by piling up post-war claims against itself. It was especially possible to do this with countries who had been in the sterling trading area in the 1930s, for most of them, having particular links with Britain, were dependent ultimately on the British market and could be persuaded to allow sterling credit balances to accumulate against their names in London. In most cases this also meant, however, that Britain had to divest herself of much of her investment in those countries. India, for example, used her sterling balances to buy British investments in India. In spite of this, Indian sterling balances in London rose to £1,321 million by the end of 1945. The transposition of the roles of Britain and India during the Second World War was therefore financially not unlike, on a slightly smaller scale, that of the roles of Britain and the United States in the First World War. By the same date, and through a similar process, Middle Eastern countries, especially Egypt and the Sudan, accumulated sterling balances of over £500 million. Not only did these transactions substantially reduce Britain's future invisible earnings, but they represented a claim on Britain's real resources after the war. Post-war exports, in addition to their normal purpose, had to pay for a large part of the imports of the war years.

But as in the First World War the only hope of adequate supply lay on the other side of the Atlantic. From early 1938 the pound had been declining against the dollar on the foreign exchange.[1] Not until November 1939 did the United States administration suspend the Neutrality Acts to permit trade with Britain. From that date the British debt both to the United States and Canada mounted with such rapidity and to such a height that it was inevitable that those two countries should play a great part in determining the pattern of international economic arrangements after the end of the war. In February 1940 the Treasury compelled the surrender of investments in the United States to itself

[1] T. Balogh, 'The Drift towards a Rational Foreign Exchange Policy', *Economica*, n. 5. VII (1940).

against their market value in sterling and began to sell them on the American market. With the collapse of France the problem became more acute, for it now became necessary to buy foodstuffs with dollars as well. By the spring of 1941 the situation was more desperate than it had been in 1916. The net gold and dollar reserves were almost exhausted when the Lend-Lease Acts were passed in March. In the same month Canada began to provide supplies against sterling balances and the repatriation of her debt to Britain. By November Britain was already a substantial debtor to Canada. The Lend-Lease Acts lessened the immediate need for Britain to export but did nothing to alleviate the burden of debt after the war. The total value of Lend-Lease aid to the sterling area was $30,000 million, of which between $26,000 million and $27,000 million was to Britain. Only a part of this was cancelled out by the Reciprocal Aid provided from Britain to the U.S.A. The absolute dollar cost of the war to Britain would have financed sixteen years of British imports from the U.S.A. at the 1938 level and at 1938 prices, taking no account of British exports or other dollar earnings.[1]

When the Lend-Lease agreements were suddenly cancelled in August 1945, Britain had no alternative but to raise a loan in the United States on more orthodox terms, both to survive and to begin repayment of these sums. One aspect of this long journey into indebtedness was the long-run deterioration of the balance of payments. Before 1914 the invisible earnings on foreign investment and other international services had amply compensated for the surplus of imported goods over exports. It has already been noted that the mass of short-term debt accumulated in the First World War made the attempt to return to something approximating to the pre-war gold standard a protracted, uncomfortable and, in the end, unsuccessful affair for Britain. After 1945 the repeated balance of payments crises were of a much more severe nature, leading to the devaluation of the pound against the dollar in 1949. The severe restraints which these recurrent balance of payments crises have placed on domestic economic policy need no labouring.

It is the growth of these restraints, the constant pressure of

[1] D. F. McCurrach, 'Britain's U.S. Dollar Problem, 1939–45', *Economic Journal*, LVIII (1948). On the sterling balances, see H. A. Shannon, 'The Sterling Balances of the Sterling Area, 1939–1949', *Economic Journal*, LX (1950).

Britain's altered international financial situation on domestic economic policy, which must raise an important question. Were not the effects of the world wars on the international economy more serious for the British domestic economy than their effects on the purely domestic scene? There has been very little historical discussion of this question. The explanation might lie in the still rather parochial nature of economic history studies in this country, or in the fact that many of the contributions to the debate here considered have been made from the sidelines by scholars pursuing some other discipline. The unfortunate result is that this particular aspect can be treated only very briefly in this pamphlet, but the size of its treatment should not be taken as an indication of its importance.

It would be equally parochial to consider this question merely in terms of the British balance of payments. The change in the economic relationship of Britain and the United States has been but one part of a series of changes in the pattern of international trade and settlements. And one of the major forces operating to change that pattern has been the world wars. The world of the gold standard could never be restored after 1918. The immense distortion of currency relationships, of which the British inflation was but a pale reflection, the movement away from liberalism in international trade and domestic policy, of which the similar movement in Britain was also but a pale reflection, the creation of numerous small states with high tariffs, especially in Europe, all led to the emergence of a new and less satisfactory pattern of trade and an inadequate system of international economic arrangements. But it was mainly the effect of the First World War on other countries and not on Britain that produced these changes. The ultimate result was the emergence of an absolutely anti-liberal economic creed in certain trading countries, Fascism, which led them to accept the final and most drastic implications of the difficulties in international trade caused by the First World War and its economically disastrous peace treaties and to deny any relationship between economic growth and trade. The Second World War was a war against this particular political, social and economic ideology, and one of its major results was that the victors established a set of quasi-liberal international economic institutions whose purpose was to bring order out of the supposed international chaos of the inter-war period by re-establishing an acceptable system of international trade and payments.

As a major international trading country Britain has been most profoundly affected by these changes. Two explanations of the depression of the 1920s, current at the time, related it directly to the international effects of the First World War. One was the explanation that it was due to 'overproduction', the other that it was due to a loss of markets.

The First World War, it was argued, had caused a great expansion in the output of certain industries, coal-mining, ship-building, steel manufacturing and, above all, in the output of agricultural produce. In the 1920s demand for such a level of output was no longer present.[1] The corollary of this theory was that *per capita* incomes were too low and thus produced 'under-consumption'. These arguments seemed to have a peculiar relevance to Britain in the 1920s in view of the fact that unemployment was so heavy in a certain limited number of industries. It should be remarked that these phenomena did not reappear after the Second World War, and therefore this argument needs to be examined very closely. The growth in world production over the period 1913–25 appears to have been approximately 1·5 per cent per year, which does not seem excessive.[2] Before these arguments are made to have a special applicability to Britain alone, the meaning of 'overproduction' and 'underconsumption' should be carefully defined. When it is so defined it will be found to be only a relative concept, dependent for its definition on certain more important aspects of the international economy.

This was the view taken, although rather vaguely, by the Balfour Committee on Industry and Trade which examined the permanent harm done by the loss of markets to British exporters during the First World War.[3] The most serious loss, statistically at any rate, was the decline of 53 per cent in the export of cotton piece goods to India between 1913 and 1923. Only one-quarter of that decline, however, was attributed by the committee to the development of the Indian cotton-goods industry during the war. The total value of British exports to South America fell by over one-third over the same period, allowing for the change in value of the pound, the biggest part of the drop being attributable to the

[1] Argued most succinctly by J. H. Kirk, *Agriculture and the Trade Cycle, 1926–1931* (1933).

[2] A. Loveday, *Britain and World Trade* (1931) p. 7.

[3] *Final Report of the Committee on Industry and Trade, Parliamentary Papers*, 1928–9, VII.

loss of the Argentinian market to the United States. In contra-distinction it should be noted that in spite of the fact that British exports during the Second World War suffered much more severely than during the First World War, their level sub-sequently was much higher than had been thought possible. Of course this does not eliminate the argument that, had it not been for the First World War, British industry would have had more time to adjust to a situation which might have developed more gradually.

We are therefore brought face to face once more with the impact of the international economy on the domestic economy. At the Bretton Woods Conference in July 1944 the Allied powers agreed to set up an International Monetary Fund to deal with the problem of international illiquidity which had so haunted the inter-war period. The Fund would make gold and scarce currency, in effect, dollars, available to its members, and thus provide an initial basis of liquidity on which a much more complex super-structure of trade could be erected. At the same conference the 'Bank for Reconstruction and Development', to make develop-ment loans, was agreed on. The negotiations to establish a mutually acceptable and lower level of tariffs were less successful. Nevertheless, although the General Agreement on Tariffs and Trade (GATT), signed in 1947, only succeeded in reducing tariffs, it did reduce them in western Europe and America substantially below the level of the inter-war years. Although these arrangements were soon modified or superseded by sub-sequent trading and payment agreements, especially in Europe, there was little retreat from their spirit, for the governments which came to power in most western European countries had ideological objections to the trading developments of the 1930s every bit as strong as those of the American Government.

The effect both of these arrangements after 1945 and of the absence of such arrangements after 1918 is surely of greater importance to the British economy than the volume of literature would indicate. Of course, with the arrangements after 1945 we are dealing with very recent history where research is very difficult. But can the relationship between war and social change in Britain be fully understood without reference to their wider international framework? What effect have changes in the inter-national economy had on the formulation of domestic economic policy? Have the effects of the world wars on other countries been more important, even for developments in Britain, than their effects on Britain?

One great advantage of the liberal interpretation was its universality. Only when the debate on the effect of the wars on this country is widened to acknowledge the impact of the rest of the world on Britain will a more satisfactory, but equally universal, interpretation be produced.

Select Bibliography

THE Carnegie Endowment for International Peace, Division of Economics and History, began during the course of the First World War to commission certain studies on the economic and social history of that war. At the end of the war this developed into a plan for commissioning a complete economic and social history of the war for all the nations involved. This ambitious scheme petered out in the 1930s. The books which were produced under its aegis are, effectively, individual monographs rather than part of a general work. They are like other books, some good, some bad and some awful. Books which are in this series are indicated with an asterisk (*).

The Cabinet Office Historical Section undertook a similar task for Britain after the Second World War. In this case all the volumes are part of a common plan and all have a common stamp. They are the records of ministerial policy written by independent authors. All, without exception, therefore, irrespective of their quality as books, have a particular and special usefulness. I have indicated here only those which are particularly relevant to the themes touched on in this pamphlet, but no disrespect is meant to the authors of those omitted. Books in this series (History of the Second World War, United Kingdom Civil Series) are indicated with a dagger (†).

P. Abrams, 'The Failure of Social Reform, 1918–1920', *Past and Present*, no. 24 (1963). Argues that the ability of particular social groups to benefit from war depends on the degree to which they participate, which varies widely, and in their power to influence political decisions. He takes the view that previous theories about war and social change, in particular that of Andrzejewski, have been too undiscriminating. Unfortunately he has little evidence to support his ideas.

*I. O. Andrews, *Economic Effects of the War upon Women and Children in Great Britain* (New York, 1918). The best book on its subject for all its brevity.

S. Andrzejewski, *Military Organisation and Society* (1954). Proposes the theory of the 'military participation ratio', that there is in every society an optimum ratio of military participation in war and that the gap between that optimum ratio and the actual ratio enables us to see which social groups will benefit in future wars by becoming involved.

*Sir W. H. Beveridge, *British Food Control* (1928). Has much wider importance than its title suggests. It is indispensable for its information on consumption levels during and after the war.

*E. L. Bogart, *Direct Costs of the Present War* (New York, 1918). Is a preliminary study for

Direct and Indirect Costs of the Great World War (1920). The most complete attempt actually to calculate the financial cost of all aspects of the war within the terms of classical liberal theory. Although Bogart draws heavily on statistical procedures and methodological concepts first employed by others, the comprehensiveness of his work is such as to make it represent the culminating point of a whole approach to the subject.

*A. L. Bowley, *Prices and Wages in the United Kingdom, 1914–20* (1921). The best attempt at measuring the true movement and distribution of real wage rates and earnings in its period.

Some Economic Consequences of the Great War (1930) is a summation of much earlier published work and touches on almost all the themes which had interested Bowley. His approach is fiercely statistical, but his thoroughness and his determination to measure everything that could be measured has made his work the starting-point of much subsequent discussion which is neither so thorough nor so cautious.

R. H. Brand, *War and National Finance* (1921). A series of essays published throughout the war by an international financier who was able to view the situation both with the involvement of a businessman and the detachment of an Oxford fellow. A resolutely liberal approach; only in the very last essay does he perceive the social change which the war brought about.

J. Chardonnet, *Les Conséquences économiques de la guerre, 1939–1946* (Paris, 1947). The only attempt at a general summary, but its approach is too narrow.

*G. D. H. Cole, *Trade Unionism and Munitions* (1923). A study of the impact of mechanisation on the trade union movement and, occasionally, on the workers.

†W. H. B. Court, *Coal* (1951). An excellent study of an industry which failed either to improve its production or its productivity in wartime.

G. A. B. Dewar, *The Great Munitions Feat, 1914–18* (1941). Not intended as a scholarly study, but a very good summary of what actually happened in wartime factories.

*S. Dumas and K. O. Vedel-Petersen, *Losses of Life Caused by War*, Part II: *The World War* (1923).

H. Durant and J. Goldmann, 'The Distribution of Working-Class Savings', *Bulletin of the Oxford University Institute of Statistics*, VII (1945). Shows how unequal their distribution was and how low they were.

R. Easterlin, *The Postwar American Baby Boom in Historical Perspective*, National Bureau of Economic Research, Occasional Paper 79 (Princeton, 1962). Shows the impact of the end of the war on the American birth-rate and raises many intriguing questions about the demographic impact of wars generally.

*C. E. Fayle, *The War and the Shipping Industry* (1927). Makes a useful factual contribution to the debate on the relationship of the First World War to the following depression.

A. W. Flux, 'Our Food Supply before and after the War', *Journal of the Royal Statistical Society*, LXXXX (1930). Shows the changes in agricultural production and diet which were furthered by the First World War.

W. H. Form and C. P. Loomis, 'The Persistence and Emergence of Social and Cultural Systems in Disasters', *American Sociological Review*, XXI (1956). See also and S. Nosow, *Community in Disaster* (New York, 1958). Shows the deep resistance to cultural and economic change which 'disaster' can produce, together with its tendency to accelerate such changes.

Sir R. Giffen, *Economic Inquiries and Studies* (1904). The first volume contains the author's attempts to 'cost' the Franco-Prussian War, attempts which had a strong influence on subsequent studies on the First World War.

P. Grand'Jean, *Guerres, fluctuations et croissance* (Paris, 1967). A modern study putting great emphasis on the productive aspect of war.

†H. D. Hall, *North American Supply* (1955). Important for the international effects of the Second World War.

†and C. C. Wrigley, *Studies of Overseas Supply* (1956). See above.

†W. K. Hancock and M. M. Gowing, *The British War Economy* (1949). A most successful attempt to summarise the important themes of the other official histories, although at times rather bland.

*B. H. Hibbard, *Effects of the Great War upon Agriculture in the United States and Great Britain* (New York, 1919). A useful factual study.

B. Hickman, *The Korean War and United States Economic Activity, 1950–1952*, National Bureau of Economic Research, Occasional Paper 49 (Princeton, 1955) is summarised in certain chapters of

Growth and Stability of the Postwar Economy (Brookings Institution, Washington, 1960). Draws attention to the relationship between the stability of the United States economy since 1945 and the impact both of changes during the Second World War and the Korean War. A theoretical antidote to many assumptions made about the 1920s.

A. F. Hinrichs, 'The Defence Program and Labor Supply in the United States', *Canadian Journal of Economics and Political Science*, VII (1941). A suggestive article on the impact of rearmament in the American economy.

*F. W. Hirst and J. E. Allen, *British War Budgets* (1928). An angry liberal denuciation of government policy and its harmful effects.

*F. W. Hirst, *The Consequences of the War to Great Britain* (1934). Hirst turned what should have been the summary volume in the Carnegie Series into a passionate statement of the view that war was a loss.

†W. Hornby, *Factories and Plant* (1958). Shows the scale of production and organisation required in the Second World War.

S. J. Hurwitz, *State Intervention in Great Britain, 1914–18* (New York, 1949). Very much a study of opinion.

J. M. Keynes, *The Economic Consequences of the Peace* (1920). A study of the probable effects of the peace treaty on the international economy.

How to Pay for the War (1940). Originally published as a series of articles in *The Times*, this essay contains the author's proposals for deferred pay.

J. H. Kirk, *Agriculture and the Trade Cycle, 1926–1931* (1933).
A clear statement of the 'overproduction' theory of the slump
of the 1920s.

A. W. Kirkaldy (ed.), *British Finance, during and after the War,
1914–21* (1921). One of the first and sternest criticisms of
financial policy in the First World War.

K. Langley, 'The Distribution of Capital in Private Hands in
1936–8 and 1946–7', *Bulletin of the Oxford University
Institute of Statistics*, XIII (1951).

C. E. V. Leser, 'Changes in the Level and Diversity of Employment in Regions of Great Britain, 1939–1947', *Economic
Journal*, LIX (1949).

*E. M. H. Lloyd, *Experiments in State Control* (1924). While
describing excellently the slow process by which the
government was drawn into economic life in the First World
War, Lloyd also used those events as a parable to preach in a
most spirited way his own views on economic management
and 'efficiency'. The most interesting and provocative of all
the Carnegie histories, marking a turning-point in the
interpretation of the war.

A. M. Low, *Benefits of War* (1943). The title speaks for itself.

D. F. McCurrach, 'Britain's U.S. Dollar Problem, 1939–45', *Economic Journal*, LVIII (1948). A statement of the movement
and size of the dollar debt during the Second World War.

A. Marwick, *The Deluge* (1965). A popular study of social change
in the First World War.
    Britain in the Century of Total War (1968). Another popular
study of social change.

E. V. Morgan, *Studies in British Financial Policy, 1914–25* (1952).
The clearest exposition of that policy.

†K. A. H. Murray, *Agriculture* (1955). A clear account of the
changes in British agriculture during the Second World
War, prefaced by an exposition of previous trends.

National Institute of Economic and Social Research, *Lessons of
the British War Economy* (Cambridge, 1951). A series of
essays on the day-to-day administrative functioning of, and
changes in, the economic administration during the Second
World War.

J. L. Nicholson, 'Employment and National Income during the
War', *Bulletin of the Oxford University Institute of Statistics*,
VII (1945).

'Earnings and Hours of Labour, 1938–1945', *Bulletin of the Oxford University Institute of Statistics*, VIII (1946). Nicholson's articles contain a comprehensive examination of the official 'cost-of-living' index.

†M. M. Postan, *British War Production* (1952). One of the more revealing of the official histories which is also an excellent summary of subjects handled in other volumes.

L. Robbins, *The Economic Problem in Peace and War* (1947). Lectures which reveal the modification of the liberal view on war economies under the pressure of events.

†R. S. Sayers, *Financial Policy, 1939–45* (1956). An excellent study which reveals the essential continuity of government policy and the extent to which that policy had already been permeated by 'Keynesian' ideas before the war even though those ideas had had less effect on the Treasury.

D. Seers, *Changes in the Cost of Living and the Distribution of Income since 1938* (Oxford, 1949). A collection of the author's articles in the *Bulletin of the Oxford University Institute of Statistics*, constituting the best attempt at actually measuring the social changes brought about by the war since Bowley's attempts to do the same thing for the First World War.

F. Fairer Smith, *War Finance and its Consequences* (1936). A criticism of British financial policy in the First World War which has considerable significance for the Second World War.

P. A. Sorokin, *Man and Society in Calamity* (New York, 1942). The starting-point of much subsequent research on this topic.

Sir J. Stamp, *The Financial Aftermath of War* (1932). Is useful for its consideration of the changes which the First World War brought in the taxation system.

R. H. Tawney, 'The Abolition of Economic Controls, 1918–1921', *Economic History Review*, XIII (1943). Tawney regarded their abolition as inevitable but unwise, since it was against the long-run trend of the economy, which he regarded as desirable.

†R. M. Titmuss, *Problems of Social Policy* (1950). A most instructive book on war. It is here that the author's theories on the social results of the Second World War are most fully set out.

Essays on the 'Welfare State' (1958). Two of the essays discuss Titmuss's view of the relationship between war and social change, the theme which binds all the essays together.

*H. Wolfe, *Labour Supply and Regulation* (1923). A useful study of the changes in the labour market in the First World War.

Index

social change (*cont.*)
  and 'military participation ratio', 21–3, 54
  and Second World War, 22–5, 29, 40, 44, 58, 59
soldiers, *see* army
Sorokin, P. A., 40 & n., 58
South America, exports to, 50–51
Stamp, Sir J., 58
state control, 19–20
submarine blockade, 17, 25, 45
Sudan, 47

tariffs, protectionist/nationalist, 20, 49
Tawney, R. H., 20–1 & n., 58
taxation
  in First World War, 12, 16, 18, 27, 32, 38, 58
  and Second World War, 29, 38, 41
Titmuss, R. M., 22 & n., 23–4, 39, 41, 58–9
trade unions, 20, 55
trading balances, 45

United Kingdom Oilseed Brokers' Association, 41
United States
  and defence expenditure, 17
  economic relation to Britain, 18, 45–51
  imports from, 34
Utility Scheme, 35

wages
  of agricultural workers, 26
  of soldiers, 18, 31, 37
  of working class, 32–3, 36–9
  See also income
'war debt', 46. *See also* debt, public/national
'war economy', 9, 15, 20, 28
War Savings Certificates, 29
War Health Committee, 29
Webb, Sidney and Beatrice, 44
Welfare State, 22, 25. *See also* National Health
Wolfe, H., 59
women
  economic position of, 18, 23
  employment of, 31–2, 36–7

Youngson, A. J., 10 n.